How Can We Save the Cheetah?

A Problem and Solution Text

Phillip Simpson

Heinemann
LIBRARY

Chicago, Illinois

Edited by Diyan Leake and Kathryn Clay
Designed by Steve Mead
Picture research by Tracy Cummins
Production by Helen McCreath
Originated by Capstone Global Library Ltd

Library of Congress Cataloging-in-Publication Data
Simpson, Phillip W., 1971- author.
  How can we save the cheetah? : a problem and solution text /
Phillip Simpson.
      pages cm.—(Text structures)
  Summary: "This book outlines how the cheetah is endangered
and describes possible solutions to protect the species. It is written
primarily using the problem and solution text structure."—Provided
by publisher.
  Includes bibliographical references and index.
  ISBN 978-1-4846-0415-1 (pb)
  1. Cheetah—Juvenile literature. 2. Cheetah—Conservation—Juvenile
literature. 3. Wildlife conservation—Juvenile literature.
4. Endangered species—Juvenile literature. I. Title.

QL737.C23S56155 2015
599.75'9—dc23   2013040369

Photo Credits
Corbis: © Splash News, 20, © Suzi Eszterhas/Minden Pictures,
23, © Thorsten Milse/Robert Harding World Imagery, 21; Getty
Images: AFP, 22, LIONEL BONAVENTURE/AFP, 13, Mint Images
- Frans Lanting, 25; Naturepl.com: © Andrew Harrington, 18, ©
Anup Shah, 15, 16, © Denis-Huot, Front cover, © Suzi Eszterhas,
14, 19, © Tony Phelps, 26; Shutterstock: Alan Jeffery, 5, Black Sheep
Media, 10, Bryan Busovicki, 11, Jakub Krechowicz, 29 (notebook),
mdd, 7, nutsiam, 12, Ohishiapply, 28, Stu Porter, 4, urfin, 29 (pen),
Worakit Sirijinda, 24; Superstock: Fancy Collection, 27, NHPA, 17

Artistic Effects
Shutterstock: Livijus Raubickas, Olga Kovalenko, Peshkova, Roman
Sotola, williammpark

Printed and bound in China.
010634RP

Contents

The text in this book has been organized using the problem and solution text structure. Writers use the problem and solution text structure to present a problem and suggest possible solutions. To find out more about writing using this text structure, see page 28.

Some words are shown in bold, **like this**. You can find out what they mean by looking in the glossary.

What is a Cheetah?

The cheetah is one of the big cats and is the world's fastest land **mammal**. Unlike most big cats, cheetahs are active during the day, hunting **prey** such as antelope and hares. Their spotted coats provide excellent **camouflage**, which allows them to blend in with the dry grass of the African **savannahs**.

Cheetahs can reach speeds of up to 75 miles (121 kilometers) per hour.

Female cheetahs usually have three cubs. These cubs live with their mother for up to two years. Male cheetahs often form small groups of two or three. The cheetah is **endangered** in some parts of the world, mostly due to the destruction of its natural **habitat**.

Many cheetah cubs do not survive to be adults.

Cheetah Numbers

More than 100 years ago, it was **estimated** that there were 100,000 cheetahs living in the wild. About 30 years ago, that number had fallen to less than 2,500. Today it is believed there are around 10,000 cheetahs remaining, but that figure might be as low as 5,000.

Graph showing cheetah decline

The total cheetah population is falling, and they are in danger of becoming extinct.

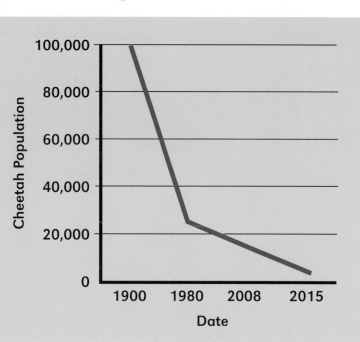

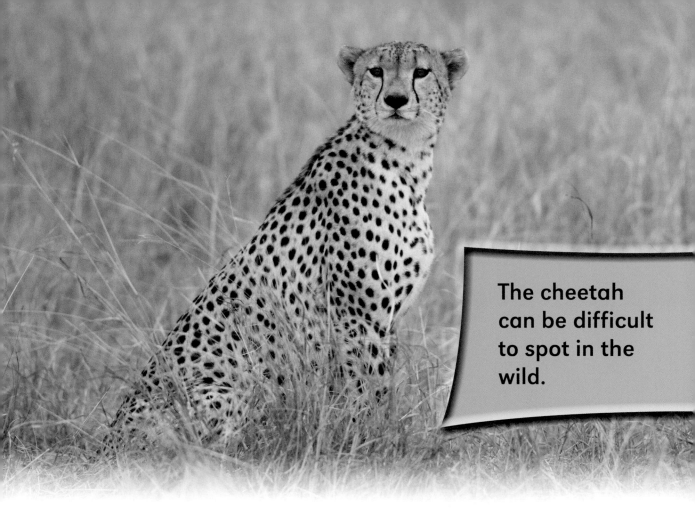

The cheetah can be difficult to spot in the wild.

Cheetah numbers are hard to estimate. Counting wild cats is very difficult because they move around a lot. They are also difficult to spot because of their camouflage. The same cheetah might also be counted more than once.

Where do Cheetahs Live?

Cheetahs once lived in 44 countries across Africa and Asia. Many of these populations are now **extinct**. Today cheetahs are mainly found in countries in southwest Africa. Most live in small groups outside protected game reserves.

Map showing past locations of cheetahs

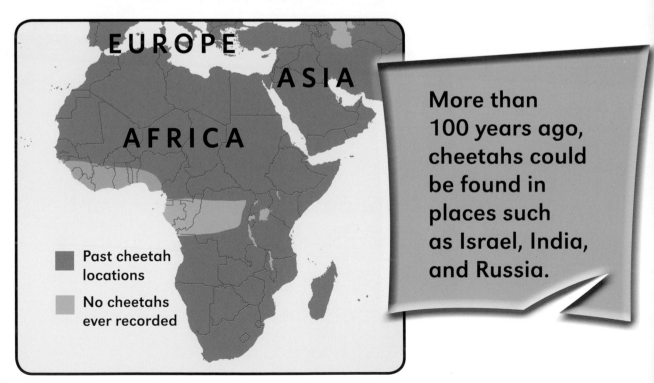

EUROPE

ASIA

AFRICA

Past cheetah locations

No cheetahs ever recorded

More than 100 years ago, cheetahs could be found in places such as Israel, India, and Russia.

Today the Asian cheetah is nearly extinct. It became extinct in India in the 1950s. The last cheetah was seen in Israel in 1956. A small number of cheetahs are still found in Iran. The largest population of cheetahs is in the African country Namibia. About 2,500 cheetahs live there.

Map showing current locations of cheetahs

AFRICA

Sahara Desert

Sahel

Kenya

Tanzania

Current cheetah locations

Namibia

Botswana

Cheetahs can still be found in Botswana, Kenya, Namibia, and Tanzania. Small numbers live in the Sahara Desert and the Sahel region.

Cheetah Habitats

A habitat is a place where an animal has everything it needs to survive, including food, water, and shelter. Cheetahs live in large open areas such as savannahs. They can also live in other habitats, such as deserts or semi-deserts. In Namibia cheetah habitats include grasslands, savannahs, and mountains.

The savannah has everything a cheetah needs to survive.

Cheetahs can spot prey far in the distance on the flat plains of Africa.

Cheetahs need a huge space in which to live. These spaces are known as home ranges. The average home range of a male cheetah is 519 square miles (1,344 square kilometers). Female home ranges are even larger at 834 square miles (2,160 square kilometers).

Problems with Humans

Humans are the reason that cheetahs are under threat. Cheetah numbers continue to fall mainly because of the destruction of their habitat. More people means more land is needed for farming and housing. Because a cheetah's home range is so large, it often comes into contact with humans.

Humans move onto land that was once the cheetah's home.

Some people use cheetah skins to make clothing.

Habitat destruction has also caused the number of prey animals to decrease. Although it prefers natural prey, the cheetah is occasionally forced to feed on **livestock**. Humans often respond by killing the cheetah.

Problems with Other Predators

Habitat loss creates other problems. With fewer prey animals to feed upon, competition among **predators** has increased. The cheetah is one of the smallest of the big cats. Even in protected wildlife reserves, cheetahs are struggling against larger predators. Despite being excellent hunters, cheetahs are often driven away from their kill.

A cheetah is no match for a hyena.

Cheetah cubs rely on their mother for protection. But the mother must leave her cubs alone when she goes hunting. Cubs are sometimes killed by other predators because they are unable to defend themselves.

Cheetah cubs are helpless without their mothers.

Other Problems

Most cheetahs are closely related. This is because a natural disaster thousands of years ago caused the population to fall almost to extinction. The remaining cheetahs were forced to **breed** with one another. This is called inbreeding. Inbreeding has caused a lack of variety in the cheetah's **genes**, the building blocks that make up an animal.

Cheetahs are often related.

Other problems result from inbreeding. Some females are unable to have cubs. Even when they do, many cubs do not survive to become adults. Because of inbreeding, cheetahs are more likely to catch diseases. Mating with a wide range of other cheetahs helps them to fight off diseases.

Captive cheetahs are treated for different diseases.

What Can Be Done?

The cheetah is endangered and therefore is a protected animal. In many places it is against the law to hunt or kill a cheetah, or to sell any part of its body. But in Namibia protection is proving difficult because people are still allowed to kill cheetahs if they are seen as a threat to livestock or humans.

It is illegal to hunt or kill the cheetah, but farmers must protect their livestock.

People are slowly beginning to understand the importance of protecting the cheetah.

People have suggested many ways to save the cheetah. One solution is to protect the cheetah's habitat. Others have suggested giving farmers money if they have cheetahs on their land. Another solution is education. Farmers must become aware of how the cheetah increases tourism in their communities. Many tourists pay to see wild animals in their natural habitats.

19

Breeding Programs

One preservation problem is that cheetahs do not breed well in **captivity**. Zoos try to breed cheetahs that are not related to one another. As a result the cheetahs will have more variety in their genes to help cope with disease.

Scientists are trying to increase cheetah numbers.

It is hoped that cheetahs bred in zoos can be released into the wild.

Scientists have used wild Namibian cheetahs in their breeding programs. Namibian cheetahs were chosen because they have the greatest population and therefore their genes will be more varied. This program has been successful in the United States, with many new cubs being born.

Cheetah Conservation Fund

Conservation is essential for the cheetah's future. The Cheetah Conservation Fund (CCF) is based in Namibia. The CCF looks after the cheetah populations outside of protected parks and reserves, where they are especially at risk.

Members of the CCF continue to protect cheetah populations.

Education is helping to change people's attitudes toward cheetahs.

The CCF helps and advises farmers on how to look after their livestock and the wildlife that surrounds them. As a result, farmers are killing fewer cheetahs. Instead, they call the CCF for help when wild cheetahs are seen around their farms.

Reintroduction Into India

The cheetah has been extinct in India for more than 60 years. The Indian government, working with the CCF, is trying to reintroduce the cheetah to India. Selecting the right place to reintroduce cheetahs has proved difficult. Cheetahs need a lot of space for their home ranges. They also need many prey animals, such as antelope, to feed on.

A cheetah's home range needs to include antelope and other large prey.

The key to the success of the project is education. As a result, local people will see that cheetahs encourage tourism, which leads to jobs and money. The Indian government sees that the survival of cheetahs in India depends on them living safely near humans.

Researchers teach people how to help the cheetah.

Cheetah Preservation Foundation

The Cheetah Preservation Foundation was founded in 1988. It is based in the Cango Wildlife Ranch in South Africa. The foundation's goal is to ensure the survival of the cheetah and help educate visitors at the ranch. The money they raise is used on a number of projects, mostly involving breeding and rescuing cheetahs.

The Cango Wildlife Ranch is home to many endangered species.

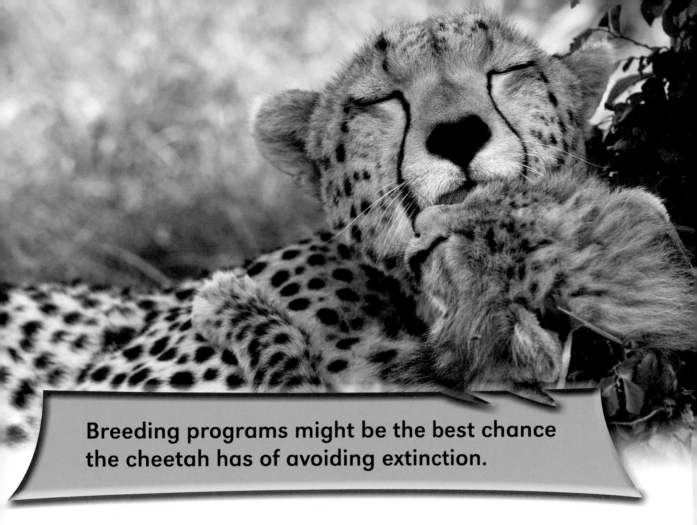

Breeding programs might be the best chance the cheetah has of avoiding extinction.

One of their most successful projects was in Namibia, where they saved 13 cheetahs that had been caught in traps. As a result, these cheetahs are now used in their breeding program. The Cheetah Preservation Foundation also provides training and education to other organizations.

Explanation of Text Structure

This text has been written using the **problem and solution** text structure. This text structure introduces a problem and discusses ways of solving it. The problem and solution text structure includes words such as *problem*, *as a result*, *solution*, *difficult*, *another*, *because*, and *help*.

Counting wild cats is very difficult because they move around a lot. Another problem is that cheetahs do not breed well in captivity. Zoos try to breed cheetahs that are not related to one another. As a result, the cheetahs will have more variety in their genes to help cope with disease. Another solution is to use science to help female cheetahs get pregnant.

Problem and solution signal words

Now you could try using the **problem and solution** text structure to write about:

- how we can reduce the amount of trash that goes in our landfills/trash cans
- how we can provide green space for children who live in cities
- how we can reduce the amount of electricity we use

Glossary

breed to mate and have young

camouflage a natural coloring or body shape that allows an animal to blend in with its surroundings

captivity held in a small area such as a zoo

conservation protection of wildlife and natural environments

endangered close to dying out

estimate to make a guess about the amount, size, or value of something

extinct no longer existing

genes characteristics that come from a parent and are transferred to its young

habitat a natural home for an animal or plant

livestock farm animals

mammal an animal that has hair on its body and feeds it babies with milk from the mother

predator an animal that hunts and eats other animals

prey an animal that is hunted and eaten by other animals

savannah a large area of grassland

Find Out More

Books

Bloom, Steve. *Big Cats: In Search of Lions, Leopards, Cheetahs, and Tigers*. Big Cats. New York: Thames and Hudson, 2012.

Gagne, Tammy. *Cheetahs*. Big Cats. Mankato, Minn.: Capstone Press, 2012.

Websites

www.bbc.co.uk/nature/life/Cheetah
Learn more about the cheetah, and watch some amazing videos on this BBC website.

www.cheetah.org.uk
If you want to help save cheetahs, you can ask your parents if they can help you fundraise for the Cheetah Conservation Fund.

www.kids.nationalgeographic.com/kids/animals/creaturefeature/cheetah
Finds lots of information about the cheetah on this website.

Index